BOOKS BY LAURIE SHECK

IO AT NIGHT   *1990*

AMARANTH   *1981*

IO AT NIGHT

IO AT NIGHT

POEMS BY

LAURIE SHECK

ALFRED A KNOPF

NEW YORK

1990

THIS IS A BORZOI BOOK
PUBLISHED BY ALFRED A. KNOPF, INC.

Some of these poems were originally published in the following periodicals:

THE IOWA REVIEW: "The Annunciation", "In the Basilica of San Francesco", "Watching Television"

THE MIDWEST QUARTERLY: "New England Graveyard", "Persephone to Demeter"

THE NEW YORKER: "To Softness", "Io", "Wounded Whale"

THE NATION: "Water"

THE ONTARIO REVIEW: "Poem Beginning with a Line from Sappho", "Main Street"

THE PARIS REVIEW: "Rush Hour"

POETRY: "Nocturne: Blue Waves" (originally published as "Untitled"), "The Soul Revisiting the Body"

POETRY NORTHWEST: "Distance", "Picture for Sale Above a Cash Register", "The Madwoman in the Attic", "The Red Cow at Lascaux"

Grateful acknowledgment is made to the *Antioch Review* for permission to reprint Laurie Sheck's "Niobe, Also, of the Beautiful Hair, Thought of Eating." First appeared in the *Antioch Review*, Vol. 43, No. 4, (Fall 1985). Copyright © 1985 by The Antioch Review, Inc. Reprinted by permission of the Editors.

I would like to thank the Ingram Merrill Foundation and the National Endowment for the Arts for grants which aided me during the writing of this book. I am grateful to the French Ministry of Antiquities for granting me permission to enter the Lascaux cave.

It is with deepest gratitude that I thank my editor, Harry Ford.

Library of Congress Cataloging-in-Publication Data

Sheck, Laurie.
   Io at night : poems / by Laurie Sheck.
      p.   cm.
   ISBN 0-394-57765-5
   ISBN 0-679-72566-0 (pbk.)
   I. Title.   II. Title: Io at night.
PS3569.H3917A624   1990
811'.54—dc20   89-45306
                                          CIP

Manufactured in the United States of America
First Edition

To James Peck and Roberta Ruliffson

Where am I? What country is this?
Who is here in a halter of stone strapped
up to the storms? . . . I am lost. O where
has the mad girl wandered?

AESCHYLUS, *Prometheus Bound*

Time's violence rends the soul: by the rent eternity enters.

SIMONE WEIL

Contents

Contents

I

Io

I am watched by the eyes in a peacock's tail.
All day I hear the voices hissing, Mad girl,
you have no roof, no door, no bed.
The world flies by in its fragments: valleys
and hilltops, doors, doors.

The evening grasses in which the footsteps disappear —
I lean down into their wavering,
the story of each blade
sequestered. The ants with crumbs on their backs,
the black dismembered bees.
Where is the girl who dreamed of being held?
Where is the girl who felt as she walked into a stand

of narrow trees made white by frost (or did she dream it?) —
the grass made steely white by frost, the air so thick
with fog she couldn't see her hands —
that she would come, if she just kept on walking long enough,
to arms that would hold her, take her in?
I remember and do not remember being her.

The towns clog the valleys like something made by fear.
Fear of loneliness, of dream.
They huddle at the bottom of the hills,
offering up to the hollowed hours a brief and fragile
calmness: glasses of clear water, windowsills of herbs.
And touch, which is sometimes not a lie.
And voices, voices
like nets cast out into the fear.

Somewhere a child lies in her crib
repeating the names of her parents, the names of her pets
and her toys as she falls off to sleep.
Somewhere a woman cries in a corner.
Somewhere a man thinks of a woman he loved who left him
who is dead. Somewhere and somewhere. The child
asleep now, the woman untying her apron,
the man going out to the store.

The world flies by in its fragments.
I remember and do not remember.
Voices, promises. Windows and doorways.
Green valleys, red hills.

Io At Night

How gray the earth is now, how still.
Pale night, mottled sky like a severed wing above the trees.
Where am I? The days grow shorter;
a brittleness like splinters in the air.

I remember the retrievable world,
the parts of it
that did not need to hide, that wanted to be watched.
As if in being watched they were made real.
The orators looming high above the sweating crowds;
their love of power some distortion
in the soul, a deformity of longing.
The rich who hung their portraits on their walls.
Seeing them, I thought it must be true:
that that which is temporal in us
secretes lies in order not to die.

Once, a child, I dreamed in fevered sleep
that all I could see of myself in the mirror
was one eye. The rest would not swim up,
no other eye, no mouth, no flesh, no hair.
And the eye that was visible, that wanted to be seen,
had filled itself with lies

like all good children.
It was the hidden that stayed whole,
though it grieved
for the world it could not touch. The dream,

of course, was wordless.
But I remember waking up and holding it close to myself
as if it were quite solid; a tablet, or a book.
How I would carry it with me
back into the world of visible, invasive things,

of smooth white walls and bolted doorways,
of families gathered like lies around their tables,
of statesmen squeezing profits
from their laws, —

that dream whose body was much purer than my own,
like the cold cliffs
at the farthest reaches of the world.

Nocturne: Blue Waves

There are times when the mind
knows no wholeness. It sees the moon broken
in the branches, the finch's shadow
as something terribly severed, black blood.
As if touch were annihilation.
As when a woman waits in her small room;
her lover enters,
raises his soft hand to her face. . . .
They lie down on the clean bed,
lie down on sweetness of pine,
feather pillows, polished wood;
but as he touches her
she pictures the shadow of a woman
burned into a wall, the others
who wandered in stunned silence
through the streets, their flesh
turned to rags in their hands.
She thinks of the woman's arms
outstretched though they held nothing,
though there was nothing to hold onto up ahead. . . .
She gets up from the bed.
It is dark now,
the man's throat
caged in shadows of branches as he sleeps.
Distance is the soul of the beautiful,
she had read, and she imagines an unknown planet
revolving in deep space, blue waves
in tender exile from the land.
Remorseless. Without witness.
If she could go there
she would possess nothing.
How beautiful the earth
might seem again from that distance.
How possible love.

In the Basilica of San Francesco

In the quiet chamber that holds us
like a kind of moonlit night, we see them gathered
without rancor, these animals staring with great tenderness,
witnessing the birth of Christ.
Giotto has left them here;
the mild attentive faces of the donkey, lamb, and cow,
their heads inclining toward the blue-robed mother and her child.
Having come to feel such tenderness
there is nothing more they need to know.
Far behind them a single pallid tree
fans its branches out in all directions,
deep into the mother sky. How frail it looks,
and yet it seems as if it's rooted there forever,
each golden leaf completely still,
small eye-shaped mirrors hanging in the silence,
covered with fine dust. And the lambs
look wholly past themselves, so calmly,
onto the massive rock that is the world. . . .
But the moment is frozen,
the tenderness kept without effort,
the thrall of birth and newness blanketing
each creature, spidering them in.
It is as if they had not yet woken.
As if a strange unearthly music lulled them,
satiate and pure. But how soon the spell
must be broken, and the years accumulate their meanings,
and the child cry out beyond solace
as his mother turns, in her sorrow, toward the window,
the flayed leaves churning, twisting downward
in a tattered slowness, the wind dragging
its great trap across the ground.
And the father, too, will sigh with tiredness,
and the donkey tug his master's cart up the steep hills
while flies clot near his eyes
and whip-marks scar his skin. And yet,
as we look into this world brought to life
by Giotto's hand, it seems the donkey's eyes
must still hold kindness, they are so deeply kind,

no matter the knowledge of affliction burning in his body,
no matter the weariness, the meekness,
as he pulls the farmer's cart over rocks
and thorny vines, pressing hard into the forest's
haunted promise, deep into the mangled beauty of the world.

The Madwoman in the Attic

All things journey back into absence. Your hands, this night,
each house that holds within it its own burning.
In a few hours I will show you. . . .
Here is my wedding gown, preserved like a mummy, all wrapped up
    for eternity.
What a fool I was then, standing like an igloo at the altar,
and my hands two fish just plucked from their poles, ice-cold.
I didn't know then what I wanted, but I knew I didn't want to live

the way so many women lived: the baby shoes of the orient, the
    long hair
twisted into knots and snaked with candy ribbons, biscuits
and coffee, biscuits and tea.
I loved when the marsh grass grew long and wild in August,
and the mud-flats as they turned the wind-blown rain to sheets
    of mica.
And the sky when it darkened, steel-gray, an old mirror silvered
    over.

All things kept are invisible. Are carried in the mind,
through flame, from solidity to dream.
Tonight when this house goes down in flames
I will not lose it. This is how it's kept, seared into the brain
like childhood, like love.
How urgent it will be in its vanishing, the fire's thousand hands
ushering each object away from human use. How I will have them then,

past dailiness, past gravity.
I want to see them one more time before they burn —
our bed, my chair, the windchime shaped like a cat with one eye
    missing.
I didn't get a chance to look at them enough
before you locked me in this room.
They drift in a haze of forgetfulness. And I think the lower floors
of this house are clouds, gray clouds,

and ghosts are drifting through them,
white hands and faces lost in a terrible vagueness.
Last night I dreamt I sent a rose streaming through those clouds.
It landed on the gown of a young woman, its stem a knife,
its bloom a pool of blood. She cried but no one heard her.
Laugh a wicked laugh I told her. Then they'll hear you.
And give you a small room to cry in. I hear the birds

crying through those clouds: be good! be good!
A crow flew right through that young girl's body
and left a feather in her neck. I thought she must be choking
but she smiled and leaned against you,
your pretty ghost-white fingers lost inside her skin.

Now I have unlocked the door. I hold this candle to the curtains.
How easily it eats them, the flames saying Come, we are ready
    to bring you
where human hands can't touch you.
How good it is, this vanishing. How willingly they go —
the curtains, bureaus, chairs. And the walls that will grow gentle
in their dying; their soft ash will feed the trees.
And my white dress is the night sky, its sleeves are blown
to nothing by the wind.

The Soul Revisiting the Body

The Papyrus of Ani, 1400 B.C.

Why do you return?
What could they mean to you now —
this flesh, these openings, these candles
burning at each end of my body
as if warmth and light could reach me?
What is it you desire?
What lack is there in Heaven?
I always thought it would be terrible
to be beyond change.
Now we are both beyond change;
there is nothing I can give you.

You have returned to me
in the form of a bird;
your wings are large,
they would enclose me.
How tremulous and soft you are,
these slow, feathery turnings
of love, of desire.
My arms are rigid at my sides.

There is so much I do not want
to remember. You remember
everything, and cannot rest.
Each transgression. Each lily
slowly opening. How so many times
you watched me move from innocence
to bitterness, from bitterness
to rage, and then
forgiveness. It's strange
how I had to forgive
the earth for not loving me,
each rock and tree,
knowing all the while
I did not matter,
that the inanimate is beautiful

because it cannot feel.
Now I am inanimate.
Your longing a flame
that cannot wound me.
Your wings embrace
an emptiness like air.

Main Street

Night-hushed, the rows of brittle windows
glitter: skins of ice.
Behind them lies the world
of the untouched: red shoes and black shoes,
shirts stiffened over cardboard throats.
The mannequins

are dressed for spring.
Each looks away from the other.
Gold bracelets glisten
on their hollow wrists.
Behind locked windows and doors
their faces are stopped clocks. Tags

hang from their dresses
blank-side up, the prices pressed
against their flesh.
This night-street is theirs;
it is their kingdom where no child
cries, and the benches are empty,

where all that has been gathered
into their arms cannot change them,
cannot alter the echoless
caverns of their chests.
Their white arms are like the arms
I've seen in dreams

that begin as babies' arms
then lengthen without warning
to adults' arms, ambiguous
and wrong. They reach out
but cannot unfreeze.
And in that dream-light the babies'

toys remain: discarded dolls
wound up by keys, reciting
their litanies of "Mommy" and "hungry"
while water poured into their heads
makes their owl-eyes cry
and their legs move awkwardly

backward and forward.
Beneath a painted midnight sky
crossed with branches bearing paper leaves,
beneath bright silver stars
and a full moon,
two mannequins are frozen

in a waltz.
Their bodies seem to touch
but do not touch
as each looks over the shoulder
of the other; the woman's cold white skin
buried in the folds of her blue gown,

the man in a black tuxedo.
Nothing scars them.
They dance behind clear glass,
above a sidewalk sprouting
small green leaves.
They dance beyond a paper

blown into a gutter,
the face of a murdered woman
bordered by columns of black print.
Their red-painted lips are smiling,
barely parted, their eyes
are steady and unfilled. No wind

touches the folds
of her long satin gown, her hands
masked in velvet gloves.
Rain does not chill the smooth
exposed skin of their throats,
or make them lower their heads

for protection. Silent as harm,
they dance while the moon
travels beyond them,
and a tomcat's cry
cuts like a baby's scream through the alley.
Their shadows never change.

Watching Television

All night the small gray figures walk and walk. Their bodies
are shadows; the light of their world flickers on my walls.
I take them just so far into my room, the gray shrouds
of their faces, their arms that cannot feel.
They want nothing of me

as I watch them pass through panelled rooms
and over lawns as soft as velvet.
Their small, perfect bodies do not falter. What do I seek
from their flesh that is not flesh, their eyes
like mummies' eyes, enameled, behind glass?

They cannot touch me, though I graze my hand against their cage.
They look and do not look.
Their ghost-flesh disappears and reappears
as if loss were not possible. There is always one of them
entering a room, taking off a jacket,

making tea. There is always one of them smiling
or driving to the beach.
The womens' legs are ivory!
Statues in a nameless museum, their voices
seem to come from a space behind their bodies

where the trees do not waver, where the chairs are smooth
as ice. In their world even the mushroom-cloud is tiny,
the size of a cocoa-puff my thumb could cover over.
Their blood is gray or black.
The gray of a corpse is different: it is its muteness

that is terrible, as if its voice continued to live
and yet was stilled. At night it is so quiet;
the world hovers mute outside my window,
a face whose mouth is bandaged over,
a face I can neither touch nor send away.

But the gray faces on the screen still speak and speak;
they are faithful, they remain.
They glide like clouds through their gray air.
The red pulse of the columbine does not touch them.
Nor the ticking of the clock. Nor the cry of a child.

Prometheus's Wrist

More and more she thought of it —
the softness tearing,
the smooth blue-veined skin, gleaming, paper-thin,
pale moon-glow seeping crimson where it rubbed against the cliff.

She did not picture his face.
She did not picture his mangled torso, his thighs.
Nor did she think of his liver,
the fierce bird-beaks needling in.
Nor the distance like a loneliness unhealed.
Nor the valley below, moss crawling on the rocks
and stoic trunks, the place where cries unbolted and dissolved.

His skin, she thought, so soft like a ghostliness
but shackled, pressing up against the virtual,
seized by its power, its spell.
His mind might move out into the air
but his wrist would bring him back
until all he could think of was rock,
feeling the relentless power of the world.
Where the stone rubbed his shackled wrists
it held him like a scandal playing on the mind,
like the strange sudden laugh — more like a cry —
escaping in a room of after-dinner drinks and idle talk,
to which all the impeccable faces neatly turn,
a room full of manners suddenly made naked
by the pained manic laugh
of a woman in a long black dress.

He felt in the rock a kind of truthfulness.
He felt in his flesh
where it hurt and chafed and bled
the pressure of the world, not love nor hate but
presence. This is its beauty, she thought, picturing him
scarring there, that it is not appropriate but true,
that under wing-beat and bird-screech
the one impaled there
must feel the contradictions: the soft night air

on his skin stroking the wound
into calmness, the night air like a dream
of unmarred flesh, the air so soft against the rock,
the strange blending of the elements,
hardness and softness, the glimmering and the dark,
against which he must mold himself,
lifting his eyes into the distances.

Stone Countenance

Carved into the chapel's cold stone pavement
her face floats above the gentle folds
of long gray robes. She lies in the stone's unyielding dusk,
the dimness cradling her head
whereby its softnesses have taken her
deep into such fleshless arms.
And she looks up into the wands of light,
the rows and rows of stained glass panels
where cruelty and tenderness bend each into the other;
Judith bathing, blood-stained, in a fountain,
Jacob secretly burying the dead
left to rot out in the open in disgrace.
Slowly he smooths the mottled dirt
above their bodies, slowly he unbends
himself, walking back into the rigid town.
All this we look upon and take into ourselves,
knowing it our world.
And we see that there is no purity,
that nothing is untouched;
not the blossoms in the wind, nor the grasses
matted down with rain. There is only this mixture
of darkness and light, of violence
and calm. As now, above us,
seared into the stained glass sky,
Isaiah's sawn asunder in the hollow of a cedar.
He who had looked out upon the arrogant
high towers and walled cities
knowing surely they would perish,
that a world without compassion had to perish.
He who uttered, "I am a man of unclean lips
living in the midst of a people with unclean lips."
Insects crawl the cedar's hollow.
The leaves lean like tenderness. How green they are,
how full above his bleeding body,
as we watch his face remember one last time
the flawed, the prideful ships,

how they betrayed the wholeness of the water with their hulls,
cutting it and cutting it, and then the small
hushed act of healing, and then the cutting,
the betrayal, once again.

Io Sees Towers in the Distance

In the distance — is it a city? How the manifest
hardens against such shimmering transparency,
armed towers looming their lit bodies over silence;
they are the city's glittering monuments to fear.

I remember seeing, long ago, a painting of such towers.
I was a child, I stood in a long hallway, a woman
at the end . . . but why? I headed toward her face
as children must in some dark way desire
to do, as if she were herself some destination
by which I needed, in my smallness, to be claimed.
But now it's not her face I see at all,

but how those painted towers leaned on their cracked wall.
They looked as if they'd soon be tumbling over.
No, not that. It was as if they couldn't quite fall down
but had to lean forever in that slippage
between fragility and strength
where earthly fear resides.
And in the windows of those towers and behind them

faces tilting from taut necks peered out.
I thought it was a plague.
It made them frightened so they hid
(though they knew they couldn't really hide).
How wide their eyes were, mouths
shut tight or screaming,

and what looked like a death-cart, black, teetered
on the street below them. Or maybe a neighboring army
had moved through the city, hacking it back
to the fragments we fear
ourselves to be. That night before bedtime

I hung my white nightgown so that it swayed
from the lowest branches of a tree.
I watched how it fluttered there, tainted
in such dimness, its pathetic empty sleeves.
I knew somewhere the elders sat up late
(the ones who governed) refining, making changes

in their laws. Rules covered them like cloth,
rhetoric covered them. But words shelter nothing.
The white sleeves swung and tattered
in the wind. Fear moves through the human body
teaching it the world.

Io in the Wind Ongoing

This texture of unknowing, texture of undulence, of fear.
How quiet the earth is, how cold.
Are those doors there in the dark?
The air floats them toward me. They gleam like tablets,
arsenic-white, and then dissolve.

The wind is a soft grave. How it moves over centuries
whose rigid mouths are silent
but whose arrogance and love
live on in pale stone forms above the soil.
I have seen them standing on the hills, the marble
temples, and I think they are most beautiful

ruined; the distance, parched or flourishing,
moving through their bodies,
blue sky flooding the worn stone.
How far they will travel from the human hands
that made them, how far from any words

that might have claimed them, making them come clear.
It is the unspeakable that calls forth the soul,
that urges it to speak.
There is no single world. Here is the memory
of daylight, and here a hand at midnight

pressing ice to a feverish forehead,
here a child's face lowered in shame beside another's
the way tenderness half-turns toward,
half-recoils from, what has maimed it.
The child does not move. The windows darken.
When she lifts her eyes it is to see the ghosts

of hilltops floating in the distance,
the liquid shapes of houses adrift beyond reason
in the dark. What does the child dream of when she sleeps?
A spider drowning in her morning glass of milk.
A white room no one can enter
in which a single flower blooms. The hours lean down

so softly on all the quiet rooftops,
edging them closer to ruin while the golden windows
burn. Soon it will be morning.
I can hear the child turning in her sleep,
the hush of her breath against the window
like the soul that knows it can do nothing
but set out like a child's dream into the dark.

Poem Beginning with a Line from Sappho

O Aphrodite, despise not my doll's little purple neckerchief
The winds are cold
The cloth burns like lupines at her throat
And keeps her warm

Despise not her silken hair which I have washed
In the sea-foam at dawn
Each gold strand coming alive in the light

Despise not her smallness
That she is married to silence
That her sleeveless arms are cold

Keep her wholeness
Shelter the unbroken shell of her body

Perhaps her silence maims her
Despise not her silence

Despise not her worn pink dress
Its three opalescent buttons like chips of conch-shell or pearl
Washed up on the shore of her body

Despise not the blankness of her face
The two blue buttons of her eyes

Despise not her innocence
Which is the innocence of a white-shrouded child
Buried in a granite tomb

Which is the loneliness
Of the untouched

Comb her hair long and long in the moonlight
Despise not the bunched cotton of her legs
Her soft body stretched out beside you when you wake

Faithful as dawnlight fallen on your pillow
Helplessly enslaved as your own shadow

Despise not the empty basket in her hands

Distance

It is the body's loneliness which is its ardor.
It is winter here. See how the deer
move through the trees
toward seeds a woman scattered on the snow.
Their hunger brings them near her,
still they keep their distance.
She feels the very tips of her fingers
come up against the air;
how what's human cannot,
for all its longing,
be absorbed into what's not.
And how quiet the deer are,
as if God had taken back their voices
to show what's beautiful
derives from what's withheld.
So it is also right, she thinks, the muteness
of the sun and of the snow.
Now the woman turns toward the deer
with a longing bordering on dread —
she wants so much to touch them,
she is afraid she'll frighten them away.
At night, as she begins to fall asleep,
she sees her outstretched hand
hovering above the thick, imprinted snow.
And then the deer
walking back through the branches
as if they had not seen her,
had not eaten the dark seeds.
Once more she sees her hand
lit this time by candles, blue flames
rising through the space between each finger.
And the world through the cold glass window
immutable in moonlight.
Because she did not touch them
all night she dreams of deer.

To Io, Afterwards

I suppose you are weary now of remembering,
that being mortal you want to convince yourself you belong
to this earth, and are anchored to the earth by love.

You lie by the river. The sky is still.
If you could you would watch the roots of the grasses,
the roots of the wildflowers hunger through the soil,
how they would cleave, as if forever,
to what they cannot finally hold.
The river's skin is cold and smooth.
When the birds fly up, a sudden panic of black wings,
you turn from the strange dream of their going.

I think of your wandering.
White skin, white hooves, how you passed without touching
what formerly you'd stopped to touch.
The children picking flowers by the river
seemed far away as stars. Allowed no rest,
you moved within the stark cage of exile
while you longed more than anything for hands.
Did the earth grow beautiful then —

the lambs sleeping on the hillsides, the olive trees
swaying where they stood?
The world uttered its unstoppable fullness.
And for the first time you saw it. You who watched it
with longing from a distance unbridgeable as death.

II

The Red Cow at Lascaux

This is the claustral beauty of the body.
In this cave of separateness, in this animal
silence, the cow leaps ceaselessly,
its red skin blazing on its bones.
It is not afraid. It is not afraid of human
touch, or the movements of strangers.
And its eyes are no more than smudges,
its eyes are like empty hands.
What is the world to it
whose flesh is ceaseless fire, whose legs
need never touch the ground?
It is its own flesh
that is most real to it. The turning
world barely grazes its body.
It is powerful and lean.
Its horns twist back like asps.
Its skin is pure;
it does not desire to be touched.
It hovers as memory hovers
deep in the hidden crypt of the skull.
If it wanted to change
it could not. Perhaps it dreams
of brown skin and wet grass,
night touching its forehead, a calf
curled at its side. But like an unhealed
wound, its red flesh goes on
burning, its red flesh
cannot stop burning.

Frieze of Little Horses, Lascaux

How calm they are,
these three small horses
journeying forward over broken stone,
travelling where the sun cannot touch them,
where rain cannot touch them.
How deeply held they are
within the silence of their flesh
so that I think it is not loneliness
that holds them, but a patience fiercely
gentle, a tenderness inviolate and whole.
And as they walk in single file,
hooves learning the ochre juttings of stone,
not once does even the smallest one stumble.
As if the earth were wholly good,
its gravity a pure and lasting love.
Their heads are raised, held high;
there are no blinders on their eyes.
Time has not entered their bodies,
it has not tethered them to fear.
Deep inside the earth they are walking,
beneath houses and fields they are walking.
The gray annihilations
bloom and spread above them.
But nothing has harmed them.
Nothing has changed
their watchfulness to dread.

The Red Deer at Lascaux

And then the guide's narrow light
raised you from the crypt
of the unbidden. Black massive bison, thick as hills,
butted their fierce heads against the air
as if it were boulders to be rolled.
Bulls dragged bloodied arrows from their backs,
harm stroking the tensile flanks
without let-up, murmuring What is it that owns you if not force?

But you were calm against them,
limbs lithe and wiry as you leapt through the body
of a bull. And I thought, whoever drew you
could not have done so without love —
each line of your body had to be gotten just right
the first time, the calcite allowed no erasure.
So when, those centuries ago,
a hand birthed you on that wall,
seared you there sinew and bone,

that hand must have known beyond forethought or pause
how you'd stop at the edge of forest and clear field,
your nose upturned, sensing some taint
in the air. It must have known how you'd listen
to the rubbing of leaf against twig, of twig
against grass, against dust, the smallest sounds
that might mean danger, out where the last undergrowth ends
and the gray shapes of the world's open motion begin.
The place where sustenance and danger
touch. It must have known how you would not
turn toward the human.

And did that hand, having reached through its own solitude
to find you, feel even then
in that early unharmed world uncut by bombed-out
buildings, junk heaps, burning cars,
the need to break, to shatter itself
against your purity as against stone?

You rise through the living body of the bull,
your head upraised, your legs upraised,
and I will open your graves and cause you to come up out
of your graves,
leaping, the size of a heart, the color of a heart,
and the sinews and the flesh came upon them
and the skin covered them
and breath came into them and they lived.

Persephone to Demeter

My pillow is cold, mother, and my little bed so neat
with starched white linens — only the light will lie on it now.
Deep in my dark cave you will not
find me. The fat worms curl, slick red rings
around my fingers, and I am not afraid.
It is you I feared, those nights you stepped into my shadow
as I slept. As if to strip it
from the window, a cloak to wrap around your chilly skin.

You thought I slept those nights
you kneeled beside my bed, twining my hair
between your fingers, your arms circling me so softly
as if to guide me back into your body.
As if then you would feel whole. Your sadness
a silence sealing my eyelids, my mouth.

Now alone in this rough cave inside the earth
I hear my breath going out and coming in
like an invisible sea,
a sea where the drowned have no bodies;
they are the voices inside me rising and falling
in the dusk. How lonely they are,
calling Mother, I remember the fields
filled with poppies, how you placed one in my hair;
calling Sister, remember how the sun shimmered
in our window, remember how the fields turned to gold
before they died. I think of them,
those voices, drifting on the seamless air,

dissolving into nothing.
Helpless and cold, they fall into a silence
where the gored, appalled love they were born of
can trouble them no longer.
And still I can't forget you, your footsteps
quick and wild against the surface of the earth.
And your voice, I hear it still, it is still
searching, saying Daughter, when I looked
into your eyes I saw my eyes. I planted

your white skin, your golden hair as soft
as grasses. I planted language in your body,
I was the world of your first words.

You will not find me.
The flowered fields I played in as a child
drift moon-pulled and haunted on a sea I dream
but cannot touch. They are islands of muteness,
islands of numbness and ash. And the basket
I filled and filled with poppies,
I think of it lying in a white confusion of new flowers,
emptied and weathered as a skull.
There is no returning. Boreal and white,
your touch floats like the bodies of the drowned
within my body. And your shadow has no eyes
as it glides between the earth above my cave
and the silent, cloud-masked sky.

New England Graveyard

This is the city of staring, tireless eyes.
How they gaze out upon the grass
that once brushed against
their flesh, the flux of light and dark
they moved within like water.
This one, here, carved
into red sandstone: her name is Phebe Strickland.
Her mouth is razor-straight,
tightly sealed beneath
unlidded eyes. Her moon-face
drifts and pales in its stone sky.
Wings that slope like frozen waves
curl downward from her head
onto her shoulders; each cradles
a small flower and a star.

I touch her stone.
Beneath a lucent membrane of new snow
her stilled, imprisoned voice
lies waiting there, still burning
in her bones:

Mother, I am a vast coldness. The dazzle unpatterns. Where are the windows? Stars swim in the night-trees. How does sadness die?

A hanged woman swings on her rope inside me. If I could hear her voice! What an obedient flower I was, planted in my father's house. These were my garments: obedience and fear. Masks floated on the sea of my skin. A chilly room annulled me.

In a corner I wove stars into my quilt. My body pressed against them as I slept.

Mother, stranger, window, night! — what is this stillness you have given me to? Are the poppies your sweet daughters? Do your hands lie calmly under weeds? It is too quiet inside me when I let the voices cease. Coldness spreads like a stain.

Why was I born?

All day, all night, she looks out
on the other sandstone faces:
Elijah Sadd, Reverend Isaac Chalker,
Deacon Daniel House. Skeletal faces
bordered by bunches of plump grapes,
faces circled by hooped
snakes. Bodies wrapped in winding cloth,
the sun and moon in their frail hands.
Faceless souls carried toward the heavens
in the belly of an eagle.
A face that rises in the sun, its rays
triumphant, petal-like, floating
above the Tree of Life.
A garden of eyes gazing blindly back
from death. A garden
of mouths ghosted by fear. . . .

For each face, no matter the rays
sprouting from its head, no matter
the wings poised to lift it up,
the crown of trembling feathers —
each face stares bewildered
as the isolate, cold face of Phebe Strickland
whose eyes want to know
what life was, what the strange
weightless arms that pin her down
have hunger for, why the earth
grows more beautiful
the more she cannot touch it.

*Mother, the graveyard is filled with burning candles. Flames that bend
and sway but do not die. What strange flowers they are that will never
unpetal. A violence of whitest light.*

*They grow in the moonlight, stretching and reaching, swaying and
kneeling. How hungry they are for the air!*

*My body slips into the dancing of their shadows. I press my hands,
my feet, my eyes to the grass. The candlelight warm on my forehead. The
dew moistening the hem of my robe.*

40

"Niobe, Also, of the Beautiful Hair, Thought of Eating"

and for one moment
she did not think of her seven sons,
all dead, her seven daughters
ten days dead. The bread
was coarse and warm against her palms,
and she raised it to her lips
not thinking: sword, or blood, or loss,
but tasting the deep sweetness,
the fragrant, simple goodness
of the grain. And as she ate
she raised her eyes
as if for the first time
to the cypresses leaning on the hillside,
sunlight swarming in the streambed,
the neighbors' children playing
in the garden, their bodies
quick and stuttery as birds.
If love is the soul's looking
then she loved the world for that one moment
like one who has no hands
to touch it, like one whose hands
have been removed. And when she was done,
the taste of the good, sweet bread
still branded on her tongue,
her eyes filled with the weaving
shadows of children, the shadows
of the swaying trees,
she knew she could turn from the world
without blasphemy, she knew
she was ready —
and she knelt by her dead children
as her long hair stiffened
into stone, and as evening fell
her grief-palled body hardened also
beyond longing or remembrance,
a white and rain-struck stone.

The Annunciation

This is the honest grace of her body:
that she is afraid, and in this moment does not
hide her fear. That as the pink-robed angel
bends before her pure with the power of lightness
she wants to turn away, she cannot look
into the angel's graven face. Because the child
meant to form in her will change her.
Because all she has known will dissolve,
pulling back from her like water.
For there is so little softness in me,
she thinks, and my hands are simply empty,
my hands that don't know how to fill.
I am no more than these shadows now
darkening the garden, no more
than these rigid, frightened hands.
She bows her head; her arms are crossed
against her brittle ribs. The lilies
should have closed by now, she thinks,
and still they have not closed.
Look how they breathe, such white hungers,
white mouths. And she, who must enter
the fear of her waiting, the door
of her waiting, no longer wants to see them
breathing, their smoothness like the angel's
steady face. She would lie down on the stone floor
and curl up there without thinking.
Until in the cave of her body
she might feel without willing it a tenderness
begin to form. Like the small, ghostly
clover of the meadow; the deer hidden
in the hills. A tenderness like mourning.
The source of love, she thinks, is mourning.
That wordless loss by which we come to see
the opening of these lilies, this doorway
arching onto gardens, the child that will soon form
inside her body, this loss by which we come
to bend before the given, its arms that open
unexplained, and take us in.

Picture for Sale Above a Cash Register

Inside the fake gold frame
Jesus bleeds in Mary's arms. Her robes are blue
and cannot cover her son's heart, they cannot
warm him. In her downturned face

is helplessness, as if her body were turning
to sky, while her face remained alive,
her eyes gazing at the body of her child.
Without any hands to touch him,

without any way to cradle his head.
Beyond her glasses vibrate on white shelves,
and when the train rumbles by
bearing its cargo of wishes and lies,

the whole store starts to shake.
Beneath her, hands unfold like rigid blossoms,
coins jingle inside pockets,
brown bags are filled and filled.

At night a child thinks of her,
and thinks that if there are ghosts
with empty hands that come at night
to touch the clean white plates,

the clocks, the bright-red porcelain deer,
if, from the loneliness of Heaven,
they return to feel human for one hour,
to know once more the hunger

for color, to once again awaken
to a memory of green and the soothing
crack of light beneath a door,
then they move beneath the sky-colored

body of Mary, as helpless as she
to enter forgetfulness, and they touch
the smooth white counters,
remembering when they were children,

when even the countertops floated
above them, mysterious and cold.

Childhood Pond

You lay among the cold stone statues
of the graveyard, the white amnesia of their eyes.
Beneath your blurred green surface
weeds swayed sinewy and ragged,

                                twisting upward
in the buried light.

And the child lay down beside you,
her mind already frightened of the world.

In that quiet noon
you whispered so that only she could hear you,
I am your mother and will wait for you always
for I am always the same, and my body forever the same.
Do not forget me, the sound of my waiting,
I who must lie without moving.
And the shade of the willow stretched slowly

                                 over you,
ignorant as ash. . . .

I bring her back to you now.
I who lifted the child I once was
up into the sunlit grieving of the world.
She walked far from the borders of your body
over hilltops and decaying leaves,
and into cities where the mirrored buildings
floated her face among the thousand faces,
she who was learning to live in the visible world.

She comes back to the still place, the mother-ghost,
the longing. She lies down beside you
as she did so long ago.
But she no longer hears your voice,
only the first silence that came after
like the sound of air after rain.
What she must live with from now on is the long echo
of that silence,

that echo is her house, her innocence, her bed.

Water

What was it that troubled
the child I was, so that one night
I walked out in my summer nightgown,
down to the sway and pull of the water,
its murmuring fullness, its calm?
Say it was how a dove,
though I thought it should be sleeping,
cooed in the distance as if from underwater,
as if to be alone and full of longing
were in itself a kind of drowning.
Say it was how when I switched on the light
I saw my room suspended
in the air outside my window, but ghostlier,
and myself like silk or gauze
stitched through with moonlight
adrift between two trees
that seemed to grow right through
the center of that room.
What in the world was real? . . . It multiplied
until sight took place in layers
and the floating room
became a kind of lure.
Say there was a girl
inside my body
who had once lived inside
that half-lit room, that chamber without walls.
In silence I followed her
down to the water.
She said she had no parents
and so she craved the water's body,
how like herself it lay
between two worlds of earth and air;
that it would rock her, take her in.
When I walked back into the house
its fierce solidity seemed a kind of poverty.
That night the water had been warm.
Even as I fell asleep
I knew my other face still drifted there,
my other hands.

Incipience

Before I missed the banished verbs
I held the face of my doll
close against my face
and loved her as she was: strict prisoner
of stillness, the ceaseless winter of her hands.

All time, all harm,
had stopped in her.
The walls were sentinels, the curtains drawn.
Where did the purple bloom?
What cunning burglar
ripped the gilded crimson from the sky?
Where did the cloud-rivers wander to at night?
They were not ours to find.
Her eyes were empty,
her gentle lips were cold.

And then it was I heard her crying.
How could it be?
Outside the walls, the trees, once barren
marble, had turned green.
The window, now unlocked,
swung fully open
and the pilgrim wind knelt down
within the room's hushed dimness
as if it had sought long to find us
and stroked our icy hair.

The Bond

With his large gnarled hand
Abraham covers the whole face of his son.
The child's body glows a soft warm gold
against his father's darkened robes,
and behind them the miles of monstrous
rock, the sky like faded parchment.
It is the child's fragility that shines there,
the gentle, flawed enchantment of his love.
Is it kindness, then, this hand of his father
forcing the bitter sight from his eyes?
As if to see is to be harmed.
So that he feels his father's calloused skin
against his cheek, and the force of the thumb
pushing down against his chin,
his head held fast against the pile of cut logs,
while Abraham is kneeling, as one would bend
beside a fevered child. How purely
Isaac must be seeing at this moment,
so deep beneath his blinded eyes.
Seeing the hand of his father, its trembling
wet skin, his father bending there
in brittle supplication, and both of their bodies
slowly burning, while Isaac's face
pushes up against his father's iron hand,
thrusting harder and harder
toward his father's pounding heart.
And when suddenly Abraham loosens his clenched hand
and lifts it from the boy's imprisoned sight,
what does he see, this child,
the scent of his father's skin on his whole face,
the world writhing blackly in the distance
as he slowly starts to focus,
the ropes that bound his wrists lying cut and fraying
on the ground, pale coiled snakes
that sleep and sleep, what does he see
walking mutely down the mountain path, so slowly,
his father's hand a lightness on his shoulder
as they slip back into the human world?

Nocturne: Mannequins, Full Moon

Tonight the moon hangs pocked
above the city's glistening spires,
the mannequins stare
from their prisons of glass.
Beyond their wintry spellbound hands,
on shelves as hard as armor
vials of perfume, boxes of watches and rings
wait in the tomblight to be touched.
The waxen hands of the mannequins
open toward the quiet street
as when, in miles of fog, hands open
onto nothing but their own impoverishment,
their lostness; white
world of abeyance
where the maimed walk without shadows,
where the lost ones sleep unseen.
The city's windows are now gated,
the glass revolving doors completely still.
The pink sheen of high-crime lights
bleeds onto the rain-slick streets.
How whole the mannequins look
in their sleek otherworldliness,
how horribly whole;
nothing can harm them, make them kneel.
They stare beyond the iron
gates, the men curled up in doorways,
the women sleeping in their cardboard caves.
Daughters of numbness, they gaze
beyond feeling, beyond change.
But the moon with her eyes of ash
fills and diminishes, diminishes and fills.
She will never be changeless;
with her skull-face of longing,
with her mouth that is open and bruised.

The Cave

There is a hollowness in remembrance
that cannot be filled.
It is like a mouth, a trembling
throat, that tries but cannot
utter any sound.
I stood in a white surf of flowers
and watched a child's face
drifting in the hollowed
darkness of a cave.
How close she seemed
and yet I could not lift her toward me
or cover her cold body.
Her mouth was barely open,
I knew she meant to speak;
that she would tell me of a time
when stone and wave and sky
spoke their own inhuman language,
and she would go to them
so gently to shield them
with her diligent small body,
thinking nothing in the world
could not want comfort,
thinking nothing deeply hurt
could not be healed. As now,
in the night's floating quietness,
I watch the distant figures
passing bent and indistinct
beneath the city's glistening windows.
They look so small
they could almost be children
still touched by the sheltered
calm of nursery walls,
those first days
when the soul was not divided,
when it did not punish itself,
not yet, for what it felt
and what it saw.

Broken Statue

The broken face of the kore
stares from the pages of my book
unaware that she is not whole,
that her left arm is missing, her neck
cracked through, her nose broken.
She stands erect, the intricate plaits
of her hair in place and undisturbed.
She is smiling. Her eyes are not afraid.
Whatever passes before her she will see,
untempted to turn away.
She accepts herself completely,
I can see it in the calm rise of each cheekbone,
the smooth ridge above her eyes.
Yet she cannot look down at her own body,
she cannot see her ruined face.
She sees the sunlit mountains,
the tall spines of the cypresses
unbending in the dust.
How beautiful she is, incapable of shame,
incapable of lying.

Winter Trees

The plenty is a lie, isn't it,
and the snow that is beautiful and evil
like the mask of obedience I wore as a child —
it smooths the world to whitest elegy,
burying its strangeness, enshrouding it in calm.

But you do not lie.
Crooked and rough, your bare branches
weave an emptiness;
through them I can see the sky
as it burns with the muted violence of twilight,
and through them the distances
ceaselessly waiting.

The farness lives in you,
and the stars that came to my childhood window
to peer in at where I lay in darkness.
How they lingered
as if searching for something to love,
something damaged and small
that would not outlive them.
They clung to such wavery skeletons,
looking in, looking in.
Black paths, my sisters,
rivers of innocence, of dust.

Winter 1881

Mary, in her blindness, waits for me
to tell her what I've seen.
I look into her eyes, the frightening
beauty of their blankness,
the smooth incorruptible surfaces
that cannot let anything in.
She is fingering buttons as we talk,
one with a raised horse's head,
one with a star. She strings them
on a thread for Carrie who is sleeping.
I want to say Mary, your hands
are so beautiful, how they hold themselves
back from the world as if they had made
their own laws of belonging,
hovering at just such a distance,
dipping down like birds
that touch and touch and then retreat.
I want to say Mary, your hands
are like the cool lifting of the willows
in spring wind, silver branches agile and estranged
above the creek's loud rushing water.

I pull my chair close to Mary's
and press the white world to her forehead:
the deep blizzard that has blown
for seven months now on and off.
The cattle that stood in calm sunshine
after the ransacking snow had passed,
I saw them from a distance,
a dream of cattle, a distortion of cattle.
They were starving, but that was not
their strangeness. The jutting ribs
and bony shoulders were not strange.
It was their heads, and how they stood
completely still; their heads white
lumpy masks, or skulls wrapped round
and round with winding cloth.
They were pressed against the ground,

breath frozen to their eyes and noses
until they couldn't see or breathe.
Their breath lashed them to the ground.
It was their own breath they suffered in,
their own breath that held them frozen
like traitorous, still hands.

Mary's hands are moving now, rising
from her lap up to her face
as if to prove they are not frozen,
that she holds the rustling of wings
inside her body.

And this is what I do not say:
that I think it was the ground that seized
the cattle, its terrible stillness, its silence
in that glaring storm. The outlaw calm
of its shutness sang to the cattle,
a diamond-white psalm
in the pounding of that storm.
So they moved toward it, craving that shutness,
that still place. They dipped their heads
into its body and made a prison of their breath.

I do not tell Mary of the cow's frozen eyes,
how when Pa freed them they ran in circles
until their eyelids unfroze
and they bellowed and cried.

When the snow melts it will seem
it never happened. Mary and I will walk out
to the wheatfields hand in hand.
I will bring her the gold tongues
of blue flowers, I will fill my voice
with blue and gold. She will say
Laura, be my eyes. But I cannot
even be my own eyes, already pushing away

what I have seen, afraid of what I've seen:
those cows, the terror of such whiteness.
And I will lie and tell her Mary, yes,
of course I'll be your eyes.

Persephone

She sits in the underworld among ghosts with outstretched arms,
their eyes, their open mouths
still grieving for the world.
They are laying their weightless heads across her lap,
searing her skin the way winter
once seared it — the air stripped
of all soothing, the wind seeking its form in the trees.
They can smell the earth
on her skin, the white narcissus, the wheat, the rain-wet soil.
The longing has winnowed her.
She looks up toward the surface of the earth
but cannot see past the gray formlessness,
the air billowing its softnesses, then still.
Each spring she is released to walk again on earth
and the living step back from where she stands
thinking she has grown strange,
the fall of her footsteps soft as tallow,
her eyes filled with shadows,
her hands like the dust that rises from the road.
She watches her mother, the young goats, the swelling trees.
Sometimes she dreams when her mother turns to touch her
her face is the face of a stranger
and a river of fire is flowing between them.
But in the underworld she no longer thinks of her mother.
She remembers a woman so ugly no one would touch her,
who was thrown scraps as she huddled
in doorways, a black shawl around her head and shoulders.
Who knelt on the muddy ground in the moonlight
smearing dirt on her naked face
and singing to the flowers.

III

Nocturne: Floating Windows

Shunless black air and gray where the windows float
and beckon from the walls. Dark room outside which the world and
    its appointments
goes on, and the weaponry goes on, and the gag-rules and the bids.
Dark room where breathing flesh hair blood
will not form into a story —
a life is not a story, after all. It is here, in this dark,
that I remember it — the church where the frescoes had faded,

the walls like mists, the mists in which the figures groped
and faltered, how they drifted almost unbodied,
hands gone, faces gone, seeming to press forward then fall back,
fading, unbeholden, caught in the thrall
of indecision: appear or disappear? love the world
or let it go? — I watched them

hover there, the pieces of their flesh like netted fish.
The pieces of their mouths, their legs.
It looked like the walls had been eating them,
or fear had been eating them;
the helplessness shining like oil on their skin.
How close the solidities hovered — candlesticks, window-bolts,
doors, the coins left by pilgrims in a jar. On the bottom

left-hand corner of one wall a cowled figure
stood beneath a giant tree, face hidden, turned away.
He was the only one intact. All around him the mists wandered,
erasing, depleting. In the distance ghostly rooftops,
pieces of a tower, its middle turned to mist.
And the ground beneath him, too, was gone,
though I could see where the poppies had once been,
their red deciding presence.
He lived in that delusive world. It was his home.
The vagueness holding just shards of what was clear.
The leaf unbranched. The rootless unleafed tree.
He looked out into that world now largely
gone, the floating hands, the shreds of watching eyes,

the vivid hesitations of those faces: push through the mist
or turn away? It was as if they couldn't decide
how powerful they were, how present anymore, how much
was up to them. Could they be whole
again, complete in sunlight waiting past the mist?
Could they come back? What is it that had claimed them?
And did they feel like amputees, still whole beneath the ghostliness,
the absence and its stain? When I left I felt their incompletion

follow me, the solid world a kind of elsewhere.
Perhaps it's almost always so. I felt in my own body their slow fading
as they hovered at the edges of the world.
Now siren, dog-bark, cry — the air splitting with such sounds
hurled out into this night, this silence.
And outside the square of window, the ones who hurry
down the street feeling half-unseen, half-seen,
as one did in childhood, I remember, the I floating in its
mists of strangeness, a hand, a mouth, this piece of me
and that, as if in time they could cohere into a wholeness
and beckon and follow and be seen.

Curriculum Vitae

It is 1973, in Rome, late summer,
and Ingeborg Bachmann is sitting in a burning room

typing her curriculum vitae.
The flames are still far enough away.

Dear Sir, her cover letter says,
from a tree on this tainted earth

the wide yellow eyes of an owl stare down.
I feel its soft feathers

when I sleep. The machines will outlast us
because they cannot feel afraid.

We who can be hurt
walk on a bed of thistles and lice,

we walk on the scars and graves we have caused.
Sir, what is the just place for human hands,

what is their vocation
given what they've wrought?

We live in an arrogant age.
I do not expect you to answer this letter.

The bird's feathers are quite lovely
in the moonlight, whatever comes to pass.

Almond Flowers

How beautiful, what is not made by fear.
This almond branch blossoming
in snow, or Rembrandt's late self-portrait
in which he watches without flinching
how the darkness is crawling up his robes,
how it will enclose him. You can see it
in his face: the young man with the jaunty hat
who thought he could do anything is dead.
The old man he has become knows that each painting
holds within its body the failure
of its dream. And still he sits
with his palette, watching the brown-red dark
pooling from the place that was his hands,
seeping toward a backdrop of deep gold.
Years later, Van Gogh is walking through a field
in winter, carrying an almond branch
home inside his coat. He knows how softness
must marry the cold. Dear Theo,
he thinks before he sleeps, here it is very dark.
I have placed the branch by the window.
I don't know how much longer it will keep,
but seeing it, I think there is a place
inside the body that is not afraid.
Do you remember how we buried our toys
in the snow? When I touch the almond flowers
they are cold and white, like milk.

Eurydice

It was the journey back toward memory that hurt her.
Slowly the numbness fell from her body
soft as the blue dress
she had left folded on a rock by the river years ago.

She could hear the minutes hissing.
Up where the sunlight claimed them
she knew they were slipping through the grasses,
binding limbs in the attitudes of powerlessness and fear.
The wind drummed the branches
while beneath them the living sat as she had left them
afraid of their separateness, masking it with words.

She did not know how to return,
to touch the deep divisions through which she knew herself
as human. And the blue distances pulling her in,
branding her their suppliant, their prey.

I was in the meadow, I remember the flowers,
how what could be so easily crushed had not been crushed.
I thought it strange how so much that is fragile
survives on the earth, the earth with its power to maim.
I watched them sway among the woundedness,
the broken twigs and shattered rocks,
the river straining from its muddy bed.

She felt the distance rising like a cry that had no sound.
She knew it was waiting, she had no right to turn away.
It was what her body wanted —
the nettles splintering the sunlight,
the wind in the treetops, the clouds.
She would go to it slowly
as one dressed in mourning approaches a field so green
it seems eternal and unhurt. She would look and look
and would not turn away, she would watch from the realm
of her separateness, her damage.
The things of the world would touch her
and her body would remember.

She saw where the earth opened,
the slit of light knifing up into the blueness.
But then there was only the fierce pull of darkness
and herself falling through it, hurtling back into the numbness
that waited like a lake below her,
a presence without eyes or limbs, a snare, a stark engulfment
whose body would undo her.

The ache of the light in the trees,
I watched it from my childhood window.
My fear whispered its treachery, its lies,
and I turned back from the promise, I pressed my face
against the granite walls.

The numbness lulled her with its lightless song.
She knew she would sleep soon, she knew
how it had gone before.
Yet even as she lay there (the trees bowing down
into the blackness, the slow freezing of her legs and arms)
she still felt the world waiting. She opened her hands.

The Surface of Earth

She thought of them
forced out into the glaring churning world —
the man and the woman ashamed of their nakedness,
stones hobbling their blistered feet,
winding roots pushing up through the soil,
some withering, some lush.

She thought of their fear.
How they watched time bloom in each thicket,
its hunger for them like a wind against their skin.
Walking, they saw how the dust crept up through the branches,
fingering each knothole, each leaf.
How time gave birth to harm.
The light left nothing alone.
They saw the long expanses, the parched brown hills
like a gentleness gone wrong,
and could see themselves already there, already tilling
the cracked soil
where they would turn from each other
in silence and in dread.

They walked in silence
and did not touch.

Once when the woman lifted her eyes
she saw in the wiry branches
an empty feathered nest.
How it hung like a small softness in the air,
and she wanted to touch it,
she imagined her hand lifting the small lost feathers
from their bed.
Once when the man raised his eyes
he saw a shadow-branch waver on a slope
and in his mind he traced that motion with his hand.
Slowly their minds crept out into the world
like shadows stealing over the soil.

And still she thought of their fear.
How they knew they knew nothing that could help them.
They looked at the earth
that would not look back at them, not ever,
and did not know how to offer it the tenderness within them.
They were afraid to look into the eyes of the other
where the lostness brooded and took flight.

Of course, she thought, they could never belong there, not really,
and in her mind she felt the coldness of their skin
and knew they would build a small hut for protection,
while the earth continued in its strangeness
like a promise entering their bodies as they slept.

River, Cliff-face, Stone

Their softness frightened them.
The man and the woman lay down on the indurate earth,
they lay on the frozen ridges of soil,
the wind pressing in against their faces
as if they were something to be claimed.

How easily harmed we are, the woman thought, tracing the man's
soft underwrist, his arm,
lingering at the scar beneath his eye.
And the man looked into the woman's eyes
and saw in them a fear he could not calm
while above them the cloud-cover loosened and dispersed.

Was it fear that made them want to have the child?
Was it a turning from the growing, unnamed harm?
The woman thought of how her words ventured out and ventured out
only to return in time to silence,
how what is uttered hovers and dissolves.
And the days in their relentlessness slipping from her skin,
and the flower-nubs bruising,
each body a battleground of tenderness and harm.
Under black upsweeping branches
the man and the woman saw the mangled carcass of a deer,
the chest scooped out, the gnarled twisted hooves.
A tenderness, a softness, stomped and clawed to something ugly.
The man and the woman watched and watched.

The child looked up from its world without language.
There was something in its face they could not touch,
was it a stillness? — a farness
like the cypresses rising at the edge of the clear field,
green-black flames at once embodied and released.
When they knelt down beside the child
who was too small to follow
they lifted it into the tangle of objects, saying look,
this is the sky, and these are flowers, these are hills.
Saying river, cliff-face, stone.
They pictured the words gleaming, an offering,

on the child's unmarked skin.
And as the child smiled at their speaking
they forgot for a moment the sheerness of the cliffs, the chafing
    rock,
the storm swooping down near where they stood.
Knothole, starlight, moon, they said, donkey, bird's nest, salt.
And the child looked up from its world without language,
its eyes gazing deep into their faces,
this child that could not heal them.

Black Figures

In Paiore's drawing of the creation
over to the right is the first man, malformed,
and then the first successful men and women.
The sky is on fire. They are trying to hold it up.
Their stick arms slice hard into the air
the way birth, for a moment, seems to conquer
death. What do they wish for, black figures
who have turned from the malformed man
beside them, not wanting to look at
what they might have been?
And what of the malformed man who was born

unfinished, unready, like most earthly things
though smoothness lies for them
making them seem whole?
He must sit apart and watch the others
holding up the flaming sky. He watches like a child
watching the strange dance of adulthood:
lies woven into vows, the need for resemblance,
such purposeful postures, the long necks
of the women touched by some unearthly light
making them seem feverish, half-gone.
Why do they keep him there

still breathing, still unburied?
They've built no walls to keep him out
and yet they will not touch him. . . .
Is he so different from what I saw
on the walls of the small fourteenth century
church in L'Aquila? It was unlocked
(there had just been some special service)
and I slipped inside to see in faded paint
Adam and Eve cast out of the garden.
How uneven they looked, how malformed.
Jutting ribs broke from their chests

until their bodies (what smoothness
did they dream of even then?) were fragmented
planes of desire and dread.
As if mere skin could not hold them together.
They walked, heads down, over the disfigured
earth; gaps and crevices and stones.
There is a dream in which the dreamer dreams himself
hacked up and tossed into the water.
He does not see his body as himself
but the beloved and feels he must send nets

into the water to retrieve it, to gather
the luminous white pieces up out of the sea.
And then the limbs are all arranged,
laid out on sand, brought back to life.
But I think the body must look then like Paiore's
malformed man, or like Adam and Eve in that church,
limbs akimbo, bones jutting at odd angles,
so that if it tried to stand it would only falter,
and must rise slowly again and falter again
until it wavers on unsteady legs
there at the quiet edges of the sea.

The Lovers

He looked out his window, while beside him the woman slept
on clean white sheets. It was late in the twentieth century,
in the days when missiles were stored in the hillsides
and the things of this world
seemed no longer called into being

but hovered frozen in an eery half-born stillness,
the hollowed posthumous light of gated storefronts, neon signs.
He believed she slept quite calmly, she breathed so softly,
a slowness gentling her skin; as if she were a wind
come to rest upon a shallow pond —
then he knew he thought of her falsely.

In the window across the way that was, he thought, the same
exact dimensions as his window, he saw the stiff claw
of a mannequin's hand, a mirror, plastic rose. . . . He turned
to touch the woman's shoulder.
She made a sound so small, so quavery, it hurt him.
Where had he seen it?—

the painting of two lovers lying in a broken boat.
The fierce waves swirled around them, wind-swept, riven,
so cold and dark their skin glowed white
and silver. And yet their feet were bare, the woman's chest
        uncovered.
Then he had seen the boat was not at sea at all
but in the air, where it hung like an aberrant moon,

black crags of mountain peaks around it, the scudding mist
a white derangement where it broke
against the stone. And through it all the woman's head
still rested on the man's clothed chest. He remembered, too,
how he had wanted to reach into that painting

and draw a blanket up, a shield, around the woman's naked shoulders.
And he had seen how the doomed woman's jaw was very strong
and sharp like a crow's half-opened wing.
But what had she been dreaming?
What hurt had sent them spinning from the world?
He could almost feel the boat's soft bow rotting in his hands. . . .

Outside his window the high-crime lights had come on.
Clumps of human shadows passed. He watched them stretch
then fade into the buildings' gray
facades. Above the jumble of pocked rooftops the chemical sky
flickered the color of old rust. He wanted to touch

the sleeping woman beside him, the way, as a child, he had buried
his hands, his face, in the grass.
As if his very skin was the slow rhythm of her breathing.
And still he saw the lovers turning in the ruinous
strong winds that were their world.
How small they looked in their flayed nocturnal boat.
How far from the green beginnings of the earth.

She Sees the Dark Birds

Here in the darkened room is her face on the pillow,
the one who worked in the factory
and wrote, "It is as though someone were repeating
with every passing moment: here you are
nothing, you are here to obey, to accept
everything, to keep your mouth shut."
Here is the time-clock, the bus ride home,
the monotony that softest of prisons,
the orders, the ten-parts-per-minute.
And here is the blur of hours into days,
the identity cards clipped
onto pockets, the silence of pale lowered faces.
"Things play the role of men, men the role of things."
What innocence lives on inside the body
that is not subjected, that will not bend?
What dream of the earth as it was
before one human hand had grazed it?
Here is her face on the pillow
as she looks out the hospital window
and thinks: those long yellow fields,
they are swaying like the dress
I dreamed of as a child. When she sleeps
she sees the dark-winged birds
rising without sound off the water
as if no human voice could touch them.

The Cell, San Marco

Noli Me Tangere

She must not touch him,
I know. On the wall of the tiny cell
just big enough for one table, one bed: orchards
and pale grass, a yellow fence, masses of red flowers.
She kneels among them, opening

her hand, hushed with grief and want.
Does she believe the earth has grown
completely silent, that it is also watching him,
waiting, in its stillness, to be claimed?
Or does she feel them even now pressing slowly toward her skin?—

grass, wind, the clouds lengthening over the dark green trees,
changing them, the alterable drawn in like a cloak all around her.
She has seen the broken lines of footprints
pressing down into the grass until it's matted,
until it's a path of damage.
She has watched the gardener lift
his gleaming shears, bright silver bird
plunging hard into the wildness before it.
She has felt owned by it, the movement of the world,
the sovereign minutes stroking her eyelids, her hands.
As now, the black doorway of the open
sepulchre behind her

looms like an unwanted utterance,
pulling her back from his body, her robes darkest
red, most weighted down
where it stares its black absence out onto the edge
of the green field. How she feels its coldness
inching toward her skin. She will place her hands on the rough stone.
She will take into herself the black abandonment,
damp air, cool walls, packed dirt without imprint or stain.
But she does not want to see it,
if she could she would not turn.
The earth is like his unhealed hand, she thinks,
the place of breathing is unhealed.

How quietly he steps away.
How quietly he tells her with his eyes she must stay put.
But she still sees it in the air,
even now she sees it gleaming: his hand, her reaching,
and the clear unperjured space between their bodies
like something breathing, being born.

The Resurrection of the Body

How they want to be whole again. They believe in wholeness.
After all they have seen — the ugliness of war, of death —
they believe, still, in beauty. What am I to make of that?
How they want to come back onto this earth

where they would live within such changefulness,
back where the *ifs* drift like spores over soil
grazing their bodies and the shadows of bodies,
the ones with flesh, the ones just grinning skulls.
How much they must want this — eyes, arms, the rasp of soil on skin

to struggle so. Some hold each other, dazed, the world
re-forming in their skulls, turning, glowing,
and the fragments long forgotten — stones held in childhood
hand — revolving in a golden light; those stones lifted up
from a riverbed one morning
coming back into the mind because they were once held
and so still live.

They don't seem to mind that as far as they can see
the soil is gray. They don't talk about money
or wander off toward the tall doors of government buildings
that once kept them out or let them in.
Naked, they touch each other softly
or look up into the sky.

How can I see what they see? . . . You, quiet one, still stunned,
standing by yourself behind two others, mouth closed, eyes
        open wide,
pink neck against your light brown hair,
round breasts, the scent of the inner earth still on your skin,
each part of your being seems to be saying,
This flawed world is more beautiful than anything
and we have it for so brief a time.

One Day

One day long after we are dead
the strangers will come
to look down at us
from their great distance,
the blue planet like a coin
from some ancient currency
stamped with a language blurred as ruined film.
How quiet it will be then,
the cities deserted except for the machines
still crawling over the soil
like dreams broken free of their skulls.
What did we want of the earth?
What did we ask of it? We turned
our faces away. Will they learn of us,
studying the few found texts,
the fragments of enterprise and greed,
how we disguised our fragility with stone,
how we worshipped power and feared
the softness of our bodies,
how we criss-crossed the earth with our wires
as if the constant play of voices in the air
could make us listen. But the trees
grew hushed, the waters more distant.
In a world where bombing missions were code-named
breakfast and lunch, where mannequins
stood in dressed windows, the smooth
denial of their bodies shining
in fluorescent light, our massive towers
rose like glowing masks above the soil.
Now it is over. Now they are looking down
at what we were — we who could not bring ourselves
to take pity on our softness,
to hold it as we'd hold a frightened child
who had woken, without language, in the dark.

Happiness

On Liu Li Chang Street, in Beijing,
on the lower facade of a dusty stone building,
a small man has turned his back on this world
to walk through the arched door
of another. He stands at the gate awaiting entrance.
His hand grips a braided rope
that is tied to the camel behind him, and the camel behind it.
Long bells swing from the camels' necks,
there are gifts strapped to their sides.
The clouds are not clouds, they are flowers.
And two birds as big as clouds
glide down in a measured slowness
to pass through the crumbling grating above the shut
doorway, weaving in and out from the closed world
back to this one. But I think the small man is not interested
in the birds' steady ease, the clean sweep
of wings and beaks. He is happy
to have walked a long way without speaking,
to have felt his leg muscles ache, his parched throat
grow quenched at streamside, to have chosen
which road, how many hours each day, what bite
of food to be eaten at what hour.
He is happy to have turned
from the tiered and layered glitter of the imperial palaces,
to have heard the folk songs rising
from the riverbank where once a girl sold in marriage
lifted the red veil of her betrothal
and waded out into the swiftness of the current,
her lips, when they found her, frozen in the slightest smile.
The centuries pass and pass. The cool erratic wind swoops down
against him, grazing him neither with anger nor with love.
He has his patience and his gifts. The mild sun shines.
He watches the doorway. He waits.

Rush Hour

These are the objects, the touchable — table, refrigerator, chair,
grease-splattered whiteness and woodgrain.
And here is the sound of the baby muttering and cooing,
background noise, static, the swish of cars outside
flashing by like an anger in the brain,
and the red-white-and-blue license plates with their picture of
      Lady Liberty —
she's holding up her torch
as she's swept on above the muddy roadway. What story would you see

peering into these lit windows? —
Mother and child, the fragile solidities
against the white wall, and the calendar where two bison
hunch like breathing hills
at the edge of the Firehole River, in the snow,
as the river, all slowness, all certitude, gleams and pools
      where it widens
round and smooth as handcuffs. The child is holding up a raisin
box, the mother turning from the child to the window
to the child. And the noise of the radio blurring

tomorrow's weather and the stockmarket's closing, the traffic
      report
that lingers there, hanging in her mind, until she sees
the slowed bunched cars bumper to bumper in the miles,
headlights on, stuck there and stuck there, and the featureless
trapped heads of the commuters staring through the small
strict windshields and the windows on either side where they
      can see
the gulls scavenging the landfill, and beyond that the smokestacks,
the metal-choked junkyards, the white aspirin-shaped oil drums
dotting the brown land. And in that noise, the child, all alone,

is leaning where the mother cannot follow,
into that separateness, that gash
where the world opens,
where pain and fear and beauty open. She leans and leans
in the sick fluorescent light, refrigerator hum, the clicking

of the oven as it cools. She can't
walk yet, she can't talk or even crawl.
So this is what it means to be *all eyes*
the mother thought in the blurred early days when she first held
        her,
this body that must learn to love the world
looking out at it with all of its small being, leaning in to where
all sound and shape and harm must smear itself,
a stain, into the skin. The newborn child didn't even know
that it had hands; to look was all it knew of reaching.
And the world leaned its otherness down over it, blur of fragments
shifting and dividing, the audible grown loud then hushed
to a sound much less than softness. . . .
What the child saw then were the strange shifting shapes
that were the faces; mouths, eyes,

appearing, disappearing, light, light, and the darkness
splintering, wavering, unowned.
That's what she's leaning into now, the mother thinks,
that slurring she cannot imprison, cannot catch —
that splintering that will seep into her being
year by year by year, in the dark wordless place of her unknowing,
until one day she feels it rooting there and feels how it has
        claimed her,
and one day she will name it, calling it her body and her soul.

To Softness

Under junk heaps and stripped and burning cars
and bombed-out buildings,
under iron and tin and plastic,
under U.S. Steel and Coca-Cola
and the bridge repainted silver to cover all the black
graffitied hearts and birds and names,
beneath underpass and overpass,
under timetables, profitability, summits,
margins of error and cuts,
under for your own good and in our best interest,
under front-runner, leveraged buyouts, arms deals,
state of the union, and rates of exchange,
it must be there like an ash heap
but alive, like a veil, a half-formed thought
throbbing its slow pulse behind the lips,
a softness, a tenderness,
a hand turning pages throughout the night
in a bare room, eyes at the window,
breath at the door, something in need of protection,
something capable of feeling harm.

Wounded Whale

What has not been touched is the deep black
hill of its back,
slug-smooth in glistening water.
And its song, still nested in its brain, its midnight-forest
    flesh —
that, too, has not been touched.
And the head, shaped like a blacksmith's hammer,
with eyes glittering like razors,
it bobs smooth and whole as a stone.
The shore

is flat and mild, miles of green-gray scarves billowing on water,
filmy, perishable,
thin and veined as leaves in light.
Nothing is rooted;
even the inland roads float upon water, a world of glittering flux
where driftwood houses sift slowly downward
and sand roses drift on the sea of their leaves.
In this world

the whale moves forward through syrupy thickness,
through the weight of its own wounds.
Its tail, raised like a tattered flag or a glove without fingers,
flaps back and forth,
almost a separate body
that longs to sink down on its own,
not quite lifeless,
into the morgue of the water,
tasting, awake, the salt morgue of the water.
How slowly

it falls into stillness
while its belly shines, a white shield, in the sea-light,
and the other whales, the whole ones,
keep away from the one they know
has been wounded.
Its death smell fans out into the air.
For weeks it has swum far from the propeller

that churned its living flesh like water, that changed
smooth edges into yellow ooze and crusted blood.
Melted down

like tar, deflated like flat tires in the sun,
others have sunk onto the shore,
doilies of foam prim around their fins.
Only their eyes have survived; mud-brown,
they stare amazed, wide open.
But this one still moves between the living
and the dead,

its eyes alive, its tail like ash in fire.
The sea makes little noise,
as if it, too, had stopped to watch
this breaking down of flesh,
this ghostly pushing forward from water into water,
this brutal, slow acceptance
by one more living creature
that only it

is permanent.

Eurydice in the Underworld

What's that sound now growing louder? What swiftness
of water, of wind?
Is it the noise of the world where it blurs in its hurry
to be held? The sound of the river,
what cannot be stopped.

Rock, water. A head tossing in the waves going nowhere.
Eyes, mouth, hairline, jaw.
Then the shore in its quietness. The shore
like dreamless sleep. It is there

they will bury him, his head, and then his limbs
now tossing also in the current,
a hand, a foot, one leg and then the other.
The animals circling their hunger above him.

I remember his back, the clear
borders of his body. I heard the sure fall
of his footsteps, earth, air, the place where world and body
touched. How orderly that walking,
that climbing toward an opening. And I behind him
thinking air, thinking water, thinking sky.
Picturing a wholeness, like a scene
kept in a gilded frame.

Now always the rushing of water, the bodiless wind.
Twigs, leaves, the soft eroding shore.
And this listening to which I am betrothed,
this listening I lie down with.
And the slow underbreath of mud breaking up as it slips
into the river, letting go of the rootstalks,
letting go of the rock.

A NOTE ABOUT THE AUTHOR

Laurie Sheck was born in New York City and educated at the University of Iowa and Antioch College. She currently teaches at Rutgers University. She is the author of an earlier book of poems, *Amaranth* (1981), and has received grants from the National Endowment for the Arts and the New York State Council for the Arts.

A NOTE ON THE TYPE

This book was set in Monticello, a Linotype revival of the original Roman No. 1 cut by Archibald Binny and cast in 1796 by the Philadelphia type foundry Binny & Ronaldson. The face was named Monticello in honor of its use in the monumental fifty-volume *Papers of Thomas Jefferson*, published by Princeton University Press. Monticello is a transitional type design, embodying certain features of Bulmer and Baskerville, but it is a distinguished face in its own right.

Composition by Heritage Printers, Inc.,
Charlotte, North Carolina.
Printed and bound by Halliday Lithographers,
West Hanover, Massachusetts.
Designed by Harry Ford